LET'S EAT GRANDMA

LET'S EAT GRANDMA

Summersdale Publishers Ltd
46 West Street
Chichester
West Sussex
PO19 1RP
UK

www.summersdale.com

Printed and bound in Croatia

ISBN: 978-1-78685-011-9

Substantial discounts on bulk quantities of Summersdale books are available to corporations, professional associations and other organisations. For details contact general enquiries: telephone: +44 (0) 1243 771107, fax: +44 (0) 1243 786300 or email: enquiries@summersdale.com.

LET'S EAT GRANDMA

EVERYTHING YOU NEED TO KNOW ABOUT GRAMMAR

Joanne Adams

CONTENTS

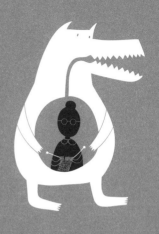

INTRODUCTION
WHY IS GRAMMAR IMPORTANT, ANYWAY?

WELCOME!

Whether you're a confident writer who's looking to brush up your grammar skills, or someone who turns pale at the sound of terms like 'future perfect' or 'double negative', this book is here to help you.

Before we begin, it's important to think about the concept of 'rules', and what we're trying to achieve. People who write and think about language often fall into two camps. On one side we have the *descriptivists*, who look at language as it is actually used in everyday life by real people. The descriptive approach to language looks at how usage changes over time, and does not cling to old and out-of-date practices. This means that a descriptivist is less likely to wince if you say 'LOL' instead of 'That was funny'. On the other side are the *prescriptivists*, who have studied the rules of English closely and spend their time disseminating them in order to maintain the quality of the language. These people probably will wince if you say 'LOL' – and if you say 'That made me LOL IRL', as I have been known to do, it might even make them fume and grind their teeth.

However, in real life, most people tend to fall somewhere in the middle of this slightly artificial divide. We know that some expressions are more acceptable than others, but we also know that new words are entering the language seemingly faster than ever (just look at *clickbait*, *selfie* and *YOLO*), while other words are seeing their meanings change (for example, *hipsters* used to be low-rise jeans, and now they're people who wear ironic glasses and too much tweed).

So what we need is a middle path between the extremes of prescribing and describing. We want to make ourselves understood, and we need to choose a way of speaking or writing that's suitable for the context we're in. The tools of grammar are here to help us achieve precisely those goals. In this book I'll be showing you how grammar works, by looking at the parts of speech, punctuation and confusing words. *Let's Eat Grandma* is designed so that you can easily dip in and out of it to find the answers to the questions that are on your mind. And by the end, when it comes to grammar, you will really know what's what!

HOW TO USE THIS BOOK

Each chapter tackles a specific subject, and within the chapters you'll find numerous subsections, each guiding you through one aspect of the English language. Peppered throughout the text, there are also a variety of boxes focusing on different themes:

 PROBLEM SOLVER

These boxes provide helpful tips for dealing with the grammar problems and confusions that we all encounter.

 WHAT NOT TO DO

This is where I get out my big grammar stick and outline mistakes to be avoided – and how to do exactly that!

THINKING OUTSIDE THE BOX

These sections explore situations when you don't have to follow a so-called grammar rule religiously, or when well-known writers have broken the rules to good effect.

DID YOU KNOW?

From time to time, I've popped in a language fact, just to shed a little light on how we got to where we are today.

I've also included some quotations about language and writing, to entertain and inspire you as you read.

 Writing is the geometry of the soul.
Plato

CHAPTER 1
BUILDING BLOCKS:
Parts of speech

LET'S GET STARTED

Before we dive into the business of putting words together into sentences and paragraphs, we're going to take a quick tour of what grammarians call the 'parts of speech':

* *Nouns*
* *Adjectives*
* *Verbs*
* *Adverbs*
* *Pronouns*
* *Conjunctions*
* *Prepositions*

You may have come across some of these words at school, and the chances are that you'll be pretty sure about some of them and a bit hazy on some of the others. However, as you read through each of these types of word, you'll start to see just how cleverly our language fits together. Little by little, the power of grammar will seep into your brain, and your writing and understanding will become clearer. So, let's begin!

NOUNS

A **noun** is a word that describes a thing, a person, a place or an idea.

thing	person	place	idea
banana	Joey	London	agility
biscuit	Emma Watson	outer space	delight
phone	Samantha	Russia	love
tree	Dr Smith	school	motivation

Concrete nouns are things that have a physical existence, such as *banana*, *Joey*, *London* and *school*.

Abstract nouns are ideas or characteristics that can't be touched or seen, such as *love*, *agility* and *motivation*.

Proper nouns are the names of individual people, places or organisations, and in English they always begin with a capital letter, such as *Joey*, *Dr Smith* and *Russia*.

 WHAT NOT TO DO

Going OTT with capitals

Sometimes we get too attached to the shift key on our computer or smartphone keyboard And Start Capitalising Every Word. You do not need to do this! It's only appropriate to use capitals in this fashion when you're writing a proper noun, such as the name of a person, place or product, or the title of an artwork, such as *To Kill a Mockingbird* or *Star Wars: The Force Awakens*.

And I hardly need to remind you that WHEN YOU WRITE ALL IN CAPITALS IT LOOKS LIKE SHOUTING.

DID YOU KNOW?

Upper-case and lower-case letters

Capital letters are sometimes called *upper-case letters*, and small letters are sometimes called *lower-case letters*. The reason for this is that when typesetting first began, and every letter was an individual piece of metal, slotted into the right order by eagle-eyed typesetters, the small letters, which were used most frequently, were stored in an open case right in front of the typesetter, while the capitals, which were needed relatively rarely, were stored in a case higher up. So the lower-case letters were stored in the lower case and the upper-case letters were stored in the upper case!

THINKING OUTSIDE THE BOX

Loving the lower-case letters

We know that sentences and proper nouns begin with capital letters, and nowadays it's very likely that if you forget to press the shift key, your computer, phone or tablet will add them for you.

However, some writers choose to create a distinctive literary identity by eschewing capitals and embracing the lower case. The most famous of these is the poet E. E. Cummings (who did not, in fact, write his name as e. e. cummings, despite writing most of his poems without any capitals). Another much-loved lower-case writer is the poet Don Marquis. His most famous literary creation is a cockroach called Archy, who had been a free-verse poet in a former life before his transmogrification into his current lowly form. Being a humble cockroach, Archy is only able to type on the typewriter in the newspaper office he lives in by headbutting the keys one by one, painfully slowly – hence the lower-case nature of his poetry. But occasionally when his friend Mehitabel the cat jumps on the typewriter, she hits the caps lock key, and THE REST OF THE POEM IS UPPER CASE. Both Cummings and Marquis are well worth investigating, and not just for their hands-off approach to the shift key.

Nouns can also be countable or uncountable. A **countable noun** is something that can be counted (the clue was in the name), and that usually can exist in both singular and plural forms. An **uncountable noun** is something that's hard to pluralise and that cannot be counted. If that sounds confusing, the following table should help to clear things up:

countable nouns		uncountable nouns
singular	plural	
banana	bananas	love
child	children	music
dinosaur	dinosaurs	paper
telephone	telephones	water
witch	witches	art

You'll see that generally we make countable nouns into plurals by adding an *s* at the end, but for **irregular plurals** like *children* we have to apply a special irregular ending. Here are a few more irregular plurals:

irregular countable nouns	
singular	plural
knife	knives
mouse	mice
phenomenon	phenomena
tooth	teeth

There are also – yes, I know this is getting a bit confusing, but hold on, because we're nearly there – some **countable nouns** *that don't have singular forms*. These are things that are intrinsically plural, such as *trousers*, *scissors*, *jeans* and *glasses*. You can't have one trouser or one scissor. Yes, you can have *one glass*, but only if it's a drinking vessel. If it's something you wear on your face, it can only be *a pair of glasses*. However, if you choose to wear a monocle, we're back in singular territory. But you should never wear a monocle unless you are a) playing the detective in a Victorian melodrama or b) an incurable hipster.

PROBLEM SOLVER

Less and *fewer*

The words *less* and *fewer* cause much consternation among grammar fanatics, and choosing the right one is another signal of a person who's in command of the English language. The simple rule is that when you are talking about *countable* objects, you use *fewer*, and when you are discussing *uncountable* objects or concepts, you use *less*.

If I decide to live a healthier lifestyle, I will eat *fewer sweets* and *fewer cakes*, but *less sugar* and *less fat* (because sweets and cakes are countable, while sugar and fat are uncountable). I will also drink *less coffee* and *fewer fizzy drinks*, and spend *less time staring at my mobile phone*.

Now that I think about it, a healthy lifestyle sounds like *less fun* than an unhealthy one.

ADJECTIVES

Adjectives are words that describe the qualities of nouns.

article	adjective	noun
a	black	cat
a	scary	story
an	expensive	holiday
a	lively	party
a	prolific	writer
an	amazing	reward
a	funny	meme

Adjectives come in three flavours: **absolute, comparative** and **superlative**. The following table shows how these forms work for different types of adjective:

	absolute	**comparative**	**superlative**
regular with one or two syllables	quick lovely	quicker lovelier	quickest loveliest
regular with three or more syllables	beautiful entertaining	more beautiful more entertaining	most beautiful most entertaining
irregular	bad good	worse better	worst best

Adjectives can also be **graded,** using adverbs such as *very*, *fairly* and *rather*. You can read *a very scary story* or go on *a rather expensive holiday*.

However, there are some adjectives that are commonly held to be **ungradable**. These are concepts that can only be entirely true or entirely absent, in the same way that a person can only be married or not married: you cannot be slightly married or very married. (The other common metaphor is pregnancy, because you can't be rather pregnant: you either are or you aren't.)

Adjectives that are commonly held to be ungradable include: *unique*, *perfect*, *eternal* and *certain*. If you think about it, it makes sense to say that two things cannot be more or less perfect than each other: they're either perfect or not perfect. Likewise, a unique artwork can't be more or less unique than anything else: it's either unique or it's not. Still, there is scope for relativity in language, and, while you might avoid describing something as 'very unique' in a formal document, it's worth remembering that the American Constitution calls for 'a more perfect union'. Language can stretch to accommodate the meanings we wish to express – but only when we're confident about how and why we're using it.

WHAT NOT TO DO

For better and for worser

In spoken English, you'll sometimes hear comparatives and superlatives being mangled and mistreated, and the results are always rather ear-jangling. If you want to be a really effective communicator, you will avoid forms like *I wish we'd played more better* and *I'm beautifuller than her*. Other grammar-klaxon words to steer clear of include *badder* and *worser*.

 WHAT NOT TO DO

Adjectival overload

Although adjectives add information to our sentences by describing our nouns in more detail, sometimes we can be tempted to add them when they're not really essential. You could add *a frozen ice cube* to your drink, but ice cubes are by their very nature frozen, so why not just add *an ice cube*? Equally, adjectives can be cliché magnets: if you find phrases like *roaring fire* and *stunning beauty* appearing throughout your text, then Mark Twain's advice below is for you. Sometimes less is more.

> *As to the adjective: when in doubt, strike it out.*
>
> Mark Twain

VERBS

A **verb** is a word that describes an action, such as *eat*, *drink* and *walk*. The basic form of a verb is called the **infinitive**, and it is often preceded by the word *to*: *to eat*, *to drink* and *to walk*.

Verbs change depending on whether we're talking about the past, the present or the future. Like adjectives, some are regular while others are irregular.

	past	present	future
regular verbs	*I walked*	*I walk*	*I will walk*
irregular verbs	*I ate*	*I eat*	*I will eat*

> **"** *The past, the present and the future walked into a bar. It was tense.* **"**

If English is your first language, it's highly likely that you are already comfortable with the different tenses that can be applied to verbs, but we'll stop and take a quick look at the 12 tenses and how they're used.

	past simple	present simple	future simple
regular verb	*I played football yesterday.*	*I play football every Wednesday.*	*I will play football in Wembley Stadium one day.*
irregular verb	*I wore my favourite outfit yesterday.*	*I wear pyjamas when I'm relaxing at home.*	*I will wear my new trainers tomorrow.*

	past continuous	present continuous	future continuous
regular verb	I was playing football when my phone rang.	I am playing football right now so I can't answer the phone.	I will be playing football on Wednesday, so I can't come to your party.
irregular verb	I was wearing my favourite outfit when I fell in a puddle.	I am wearing my smart clothes right now so I can't get dirty.	I will be wearing my old trainers when we do the Mud Run tomorrow so that I don't ruin my new ones.

	past perfect	present perfect	future perfect
regular verb	*I had played in every match that season, so I expected to play in last Saturday's game as well.*	*I have played 16 times this season.*	*I hope that by the end of the season I will have played at least 20 matches.*
irregular verb	*I had worn my favourite jeans so much that holes started to appear in them.*	*My mum is annoyed that I haven't worn the new clothes she bought me.*	*By the end of the month I will have worn my new trainers for 31 days in a row.*

	past perfect continuous	present perfect continuous	future perfect continuous
regular verb	*I had been playing all morning, so I was tired in the afternoon.*	*I have been playing football for almost all my life, so I know a lot about the game.*	*By next year, I will have been playing football for 20 years!*
irregular verb	*I had been wearing high heels all day, so when I took them off my feet were sore.*	*I have been wearing sandals with socks all my life, despite my friends' sniggers at my dress sense.*	*If I don't change them soon, I will have been wearing the same underwear for 24 hours!*

By looking at these examples, we can deduce a few key guidelines for thinking about tenses. The first three describe the past, present and future in a very simple way, as their names suggest. Continuous tenses focus on the *happening* of an action at a particular time, whether in the past, present or future. Perfect tenses allow us to describe an action that started in the past and either continues up to the present moment or has an impact on the present moment in some way. If you say *I've worked there for six years*, we will assume you still work there; if you say *I've seen every episode of The Simpsons*, we'll know that, although you're not watching it right now, there's a present reason for your saying this. (Perhaps we've all been admiring the accuracy of your Bart Simpson impression and you're explaining why it's so true to life.)

In English, it's easy to work out the past and perfect form of any regular verb, as they both end in *-ed*. If the infinitive is *play*, the past is *played* and the perfect form (also known as the past participle) is also *played*. Life gets a little more complicated with the irregular verbs, as these don't follow the rules, and so you just have to learn them. You'll find a list of some of the most frequently used irregular verbs in English at the back of the book, in Appendix 3.

WHAT NOT TO DO

Mixing up your verb forms

Most of us feel naturally confident at choosing the tense that best suits our needs, but there are a few traps for the unwary, particularly when different verbs have similar past forms. One of the most common mix-ups is between *bought* and *brought*.

	wrong	right
bought = past and past participle of *buy*	*I was planning to make a cake, so I brought all the ingredients at the supermarket.*	*I was planning to make a cake, so I bought all the ingredients at the supermarket.*

	wrong	**right**
brought = past and past participle of *bring*	I made a cake yesterday and I bought it to school this morning.	I made a cake yesterday and I brought it to school this morning.

The reason these two verbs get swapped so frequently is that quite often the actions of bringing and buying are closely related and happen at almost the same time. You *bought* the ingredients at the shop, and then you *brought* them home. So it's quite understandable that sometimes we reach for the wrong word. However, if you can train yourself to choose the correct word from these two options, your writing and your speech will be more polished – and so will your grammar halo.

PROBLEM SOLVER

Lay and *lie*

Lay and *lie* are another pair of words that confuse the grammar newbie and infuriate the grammar stickler. They are so similar and they both appear to mean the same thing – so what's the catch?

The reason we have two verbs for the action of putting a thing in a horizontal position is because English verbs come in two different types. **Transitive verbs** happen to a thing – in grammatical terminology, they are used with an object. The following sentences all contain transitive verbs, preceded by a subject and followed by an object:

I love you.
She invited him into the room.
Will you tell me a secret?

Intransitive verbs do not have an object.

They only need a subject, as the following examples show:

I walked to work this morning.
We cried with laughter.
He moves so gracefully.

Generally we don't need to think too hard about these different types of verbs, but *lay* and *lie* trip us up sometimes because they are so close to each other in meaning.

Lay is a transitive verb: you do it to a thing. Hens *lay eggs*; Paul Young sang that wherever he *lays his hat*, that's his home; and at night we *lay our heads* on our pillows.

Lie is an intransitive verb, so it doesn't have an object. Hens don't *lie* down at night – they perch; last week I found a £20 note *lying* on the ground (I really did!); and at night I sometimes *lie* awake in bed worrying about grammar.

One of the reasons these two verbs are confusing is that the past form of *lie* is *lay*. It's as if the language gods were deliberately plotting to bamboozle us – or, at the very least, to keep the authors of grammar books in business.

Here are both verbs in sentences showing their present, past and perfect forms:

	present	past	perfect
transitive verb	*My hen lays eggs.*	*Last week my hen laid a golden egg.*	*She has laid normal eggs ever since (which is a shame).*
	I lay my book down on the table every night before I go to bed.	*I laid my book down on the table before I went to bed.*	*I have laid my book down somewhere and I don't know where it is.*

	present	past	perfect
intransitive verb	*Susie lies in the garden when it's hot.*	*Susie lay on the beach to soak up the sun last weekend.*	*Susie needs to put more sun cream on as she's lain in the sun all morning.*
	I lie in bed every night.	*I lay in bed last night.*	*It's Saturday, so I've lain in bed all morning.*

Getting these two verbs clear in your mind and in your writing will mark you out as someone who really knows the *lie* of the land when it comes to the English language.

DID YOU KNOW?

Split infinitives

If you tell your friends you're brushing up your grammar skills, one of them is bound to say something about split infinitives. As we've seen, infinitives in English are formed from two words: *to* and the verb itself. This makes English different from many other languages: when we say *to love* in English, the French say *aimer*, the Germans say *lieben* and the ancient Romans, if they were still with us today, would say *amare*. Because in Latin, as in so many other languages, infinitives simply cannot be split, this led some grammarians to decide that English infinitives should also never be split, and it's a 'rule' that has floated around the grammar world for centuries.

However, if you stop to think about a few examples where we blithely split infinitives, it quickly becomes clear that 'fixing' the split infinitives can often lead to a less satisfactory result:

phrase with split infinitive	'fixed' version
to boldly go where no one has gone before	to go boldly where no one has gone before
the price of lobster is expected to more than double next year	the price of lobster is expected more than to double next year

The first, famous example loses its rhetorical power in the 'fixed' version, while the second becomes almost nonsensical. Therefore, the split infinitive is officially not a problem. Go ahead and feel free to boldly split infinitives whenever it feels like the right thing to do!

ADVERBS

An **adverb** is a word that describes the characteristics of a verb – it tells us *how* the verb is happening. In the sentence *He drove quickly to the cinema*, *quickly* is an adverb that adds information to the verb *drove*. If we change the adverb, we change the meaning of the sentence. For example, we could say *He drove slowly* or *He drove reluctantly* or *He drove recklessly*.

Adverbs have great descriptive power, as the preceding examples have demonstrated, and they can give us information about many different things. As well as telling us *how* something happens, they can also describe *where*, *when* and *to what degree* it happens. Here are some examples of the huge range of adverbs at our disposal:

how	when	where	to what degree
carefully	after	abroad	extremely
cleverly	before	everywhere	not

eagerly	daily	here	quite
quickly	never	inside	rather
reliably	often	there	really
slowly	today	underground	slightly
wildly	tomorrow	upstairs	very
passionately	now	outside	somewhat
thoughtfully	weekly	near	moderately
energetically	sometimes	far	fairly

Once you become aware of just how many adverbs there are, you'll realise that we *generally* use them in *almost* every sentence. Still, if you get *totally* carried away with adverbs, your prose may *gradually* start to feel *slightly* heavy. So, just as with adjectives, you might want to *gently* prune them down a bit if you feel your writing is becoming too florid.

Adverbs are guilty until proven innocent. **99**
Howard Ogden

✗ WHAT NOT TO DO

Double trouble with double negatives

A double negative occurs when you use two negative words that combine to make a positive statement. There are times when using a double negative in a sentence can be highly effective, because it serves to underline an emotional process. If you say *I do not disagree that Christmas is a jolly time of year*, you are implying that although you know this, you have some reservations about taking part in the merriment yourself – or, possibly, that you don't want to compete in the Best Worst Christmas Jumper Competition yet again. This subtle shade of meaning is entirely lost in the 'straighter' version of the sentence, which would be simply *I agree that Christmas is a jolly time of year*.

Sometimes you'll hear double negative structures being used incorrectly: for example, if someone gets into trouble and says *I didn't do nothing*, they are using two negatives where one would do. The correct way to proclaim their innocence would be to say *I didn't do anything* or the slightly less natural *I did nothing*: both of these sentences contain only one negative element.

Double negative structures can convey complex shades of meaning, but they can also be confusing, or at least rather time-consuming to interpret. They are best used sparingly, in sentences where you feel the overall result of such a sentence structure will *not* be *negative*.

WHAT NOT TO DO

Mixing up adjectives and adverbs

Adverbs that describe *how* an action happens are usually easy to spot, because most of them end with *-ly*. So if we compare a few adjectives and adverbs, it's the *-ly* ending that lets us tell them apart:

adjective	adverb
a slow driver	he drives slowly
a wonderful choir	they sing wonderfully
a stern teacher	the teacher spoke sternly
a graceful dancer	she danced gracefully
a lazy cat	the cat sat lazily

However, some adverbs are irregular and don't follow the *-ly* pattern:

adjective	adverb
a fast driver	*he drives fast*
a good choir	*they sing well*
a late student	*he arrived late*
a straight line	*he arrived late*
a daily exercise routine	*he exercised daily*

This can trick us into choosing the wrong word sometimes. If somebody asks you how you are, it's increasingly popular to say *I'm good, thanks*, but the correct reply should really be *I'm well, thanks*, because *well* is the adverb acting on the verb *to be*. Football managers sometimes say *The boys played good*, but what they ought to say is *The boys played well* or *It was a good match*. This kind of mix-up is perfectly acceptable in informal English, and if you go around correcting people who say they're good when you ask them how they're feeling, you'll probably find yourself with fewer friends to pose this question to in the long run. However, in a formal setting like a job interview, you will come across much better if you can select the right word and say that *you're well*, and your *journey was good*.

Choosing the correct adjective or adverb for your sentences will ensure that your *English* is *good* and that you *express* yourself *well*!

PRONOUNS

A **pronoun** is a word that takes the place of a noun. In the sentence *Peter came back because he had forgotten his hat*, the words *he* and *his* are pronouns which save us from having to use Peter's name again. Pronouns help us to avoid repetition and wordiness, and they make it easier for people to understand what we mean. Here's an overview of some of the most commonly used **pronouns** in English:

personal pronouns		possessive pronouns	reflexive pronouns
subject pronouns	object pronouns		
I	me	mine	myself
you	you	yours	yourself
he	him	his	himself
she	her	hers	herself

it	it	its	itself
we	us	ours	ourselves
they	them	theirs	themselves

 When I was a child, my English teacher looked at me and said, 'Name two pronouns.'

I replied, 'Who? Me?'

✗ WHAT NOT TO DO

Me and him

Sometimes it's easy to get tangled up when we're using subject and object pronouns. I can remember being corrected as a child when I said something like *Me and James went to the circus*; a teacher would swiftly intervene and say *James and I went to the circus*. (Even though I *knew* the teacher hadn't been to the circus with my brother. Teachers say the strangest things sometimes.)

This experience is a common one, and it has left many English speakers deeply uneasy about ever using the word *me* to talk about these kinds of shared experience. We know we should put the other person first – it's only polite, after all – and we have the feeling that the word *me* is somehow not quite acceptable.

The key here is to consider who is the *subject* of the sentence, and who (if anyone) is the *object*. *James and I went to the circus* is correct because *James and I* are both the subjects of the sentence. One trick is to see how the sentence works if you take the other person away. You would never say *Me went to the circus*, so this is a good clue that you shouldn't say *James and me went to the circus*.

Likewise, if you find yourself saying *This is strictly between you and I*, just stop for a minute and ask yourself where the subject and the object are. In this sentence, *This* is the subject, and the two people are the object, so the object pronouns *you* and *me* are the correct choice. The correct sentence is thus *This is strictly between you and me*.

 PROBLEM SOLVER

The gender-free third-person pronoun

We face a problem in English when we're referring to a generic individual person whose gender we don't know. Imagine, for example, that you find a hat left behind in your garden after hosting a summer barbecue party. You need to find out who it belongs to. It's easy enough, if you have enough time and patience, to ask everybody directly *Did you leave your hat in my garden?* What's harder is describing the problem in general. Here are the options that face you:

Somebody left his hat in my garden.	The problem with this is that the hat-leaver may have been a woman – you just don't know.
Somebody left her hat in my garden.	Now we have the opposite problem – what if the forgetful person was male?
Somebody left his or her hat in my garden.	This covers both possibilities, but after a few occurrences – If you know whose hat it is, please can you tell him or her so he or she can collect it? – it becomes exceedingly tiresome.

All three examples are grammatically correct but functionally unsatisfactory. They either exclude half the population or create wordy roadblocks at every turn. This leaves us with only one useful solution:

> *Somebody left their hat in my garden. If you know who it is, please can you tell them?*

Some grammar lovers object to this usage, on the grounds that it uses a plural pronoun to refer to an individual person. However, this practice dates back many centuries, and it is now widely viewed to be the best solution to the problem. If anyone complains about your use of this form, be sure to tell *them* you read about it here!

THINKING OUTSIDE THE BOX

Moving beyond 'he' and 'she'

The current 'standard' way of using the English language forces us to decide very quickly whether a person should be referred to as 'he' or 'she', but for some people, this binary division into a male or a female identity just doesn't feel appropriate, and could even be seen as offensive.

People who identify as transgender or as neither gender sometimes choose to use a pronoun that allows them to be addressed without being confined by the standard male and female definitions. At present, there are numerous pronoun options in use, such as 'they', 'ze' or simply using the person's name instead of a pronoun. This is a good example of the way that society and language evolve together, and it's likely that we will become used to hearing a much wider range of pronouns in the next few years.

THINKING OUTSIDE THE BOX

Personalised pronouns

Not all writers respect the commonly accepted roles pronouns play in our lives. When Julius Caesar was writing his memoirs in the first century BC, he chose to describe his own actions entirely in the third person. Gertrude Stein took a slightly different approach in a book published in 1933: in *The Autobiography of Alice B. Toklas,* she writes about herself in the third person by taking on the voice of her lover Alice, but she also drops her own full name into the text far more often than feels natural, creating a strangely formal effect.

Another way to intrigue your readers is to adopt a plural pronoun for your narrators. Karen Joy Fowler's 2004 novel *The Jane Austen Book Club* is narrated by six people writing with a single voice, as *we*, which captures the sense of a group's shared experience in a subtle but memorable way.

And in our real lives, it's not uncommon to hear Queen Elizabeth use the word we to refer to herself. This royal 'we' dates back almost a thousand years in England – but it is not recommended unless you're a monarch, as you can sound rather silly referring to yourself in the plural!

So far in this section, we've focused only on **personal pronouns**. Now it's time to look at more varieties of pronoun.

Interrogative pronouns are the words we use to ask questions about people and things:

- *Who* brought the hummus to the barbecue?

- *Whose* hat is in the garden?

- *What* is that in the hummus?

- *Which* recipe did you use?

PROBLEM SOLVER

Who and *whom*

The words *who* and *whom* can trip us up sometimes. The rules of formal English tell us that *who* applies to the subject of a sentence, and *whom* to the object. *Whom* is also used after a preposition. So if we follow these rules, we come up with examples like the following:

Who's there? (In this case, *who* is the subject.)

Whom do you think we should vote for? (In this case, *whom* refers to the object that *we* – the subject – will be voting for.)

To whom am I speaking? (Here, *whom* follows the preposition *to*.)

However, the word *whom* is falling increasingly out of use, and most people today would say and write *Who do you think we should vote for?*

Nowadays you are only likely to encounter the word *whom* in very formal documents, and in well-known phrases such as *Who did what to whom?* and *To whom it may concern*. This is one of those problems that actually isn't a problem any more. Which makes a nice change.

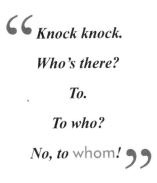

> **Knock knock.**
>
> **Who's there?**
>
> **To.**
>
> **To who?**
>
> **No, to** whom*!*

Relative pronouns appear before relative clauses in sentences like *She's the first girl* **who** *made me cry*. The relative pronouns in English are *that*, *which*, *who*, *whom* and *whose*.

PROBLEM SOLVER

That and *which*

The words *that* and *which* can often be used interchangeably – but not always. In the following sentence, both *that* and *which* are acceptable:

*She pointed at the dog **that was barking** and said, 'Can't anyone make that dog be quiet?'*

*She pointed at the dog **which was barking** and said, 'Can't anyone make that dog be quiet?'*

The clause in bold text in these sentences is known as a restrictive relative clause, which means that it contains information that is essential to the noun that comes before it. If you remove the part in bold, the sentences lose a lot of their meaning – without the clause about the dog's barking, they fail to convey the information the writer intended.

Now let's look at another sentence:

She pointed at the dog, **which was barking,** *and said, 'He's the one – let's take him home with us.'*

In this example, the words in bold add information to the sentence but they do not define it. You could remove the section in bold and we would still know what was going on. This is an example of a non-restrictive relative clause. Non-restrictive clauses are always surrounded by commas (or dashes or parentheses), and they never begin with the word *that*. If you try saying this sentence with *that* instead of *which*, you'll hear straight away that it doesn't make sense.

So the simplest solution to the problem is always to use *which* if you're in doubt. An even better solution is to ask yourself whether the clause adds vital information to the sentence (in which case you can use *that* or *which*) or whether it simply adds additional information to the sentence (in which case you will need *which*).

CONJUNCTIONS

A **conjunction** is a word that connects groups of words together. Here's a selection of some of the most frequently used English conjunctions:

or while before and as nor
except after where once but
although because since until
whether though now when
so unless like than that if

THINKING OUTSIDE THE BOX

And another thing...

Conjunctions do not cause people many problems when they are writing, because the meanings of these words are so clear that we use them every day without making any mistakes. There is, however, one bugbear among grammar purists, which we'll address here: this is the practice of starting a sentence with a conjunction. Somebody somewhere once decided that beginning a sentence with *and*, *but*, *so* or any other conjunction was not good English. *However*, many great writers throughout history have flouted this particular non-law in order to give some of their sentences a greater dramatic effect. *And* it's something you may have noticed I do a lot myself throughout this book. *So* if anyone corrects you for doing this, you can tell them it's not actually a mistake. *But* it can get a bit wearing if you do it all the time, so it's best to save it for occasions when you feel it will really help you to express yourself.

 WHAT NOT TO DO

Than and *then*

This is one of those word pairs that sound almost the same when we're speaking quickly, and so it's easy to write the wrong word when we're pressed for time or concentration. The word *than* is used for comparisons, such as *I'd rather have a starter than a main course.* The word *then* refers to time, as in *I'd rather have a starter, then a main course.*

To drive home the message of just how important it is to choose the correct one of these two words, consider the following sentences:

I'd rather read, ***then*** *watch TV.*

I'd rather read ***than*** *watch TV.*

*I'd rather canoe, **then** go bungee jumping.*

*I'd rather canoe **than** go bungee jumping.*

· · ·

*I'd prefer to order the double cheeseburger, **then** order the steak and chips.*

*I'd prefer to order the double cheeseburger **than** order the steak and chips.*

It's a small word, but it can make a big difference.

PREPOSITIONS

A **preposition** is a word that describes a relationship or direction between two elements of a sentence. Here's an overview of some of the links prepositions can create:

time	*after school*	*before 3 p.m.*	*on Monday*
place	*at home*	*in bed*	*on the table*
direction	*into the sea*	*over my head*	*to work*
manner	*by car*	*on foot*	*among others*
other	*because of*	*in case of*	*instead of*

Prepositions are highly useful words, as this famous joking sentence demonstrates (thanks, Dad):

> ❝ *Mummy, what did you bring that book that I didn't want to be read to out of about 'Down Under' up for?* ❞

THINKING OUTSIDE THE BOX

Deciding which word to end a sentence with

The most famous grammar pronouncement about prepositions is that a preposition is a word you shouldn't end a sentence with. (See what happened there?) A grammar traditionalist would recast what I've just written as *A preposition is a word with which you should not end a sentence*. This is another so-called rule that can be safely ignored, just like the one mentioned previously concerning conjunctions at the start of sentences.

Some sentences simply do not work if you recast them to avoid the preposition appearing at the end. *Who are you looking at?* becomes *At whom are you looking? What are you thinking about?* becomes *About what are you thinking?* Neither of these sentences would be appropriate in everyday life – and, in fact, if you used them, your conversational partner might well ask you *At what are you playing?* In short, if a sentence sounds good with a preposition at the end, trust your instinct and run with it. Using a preposition at the end of a sentence is something the grammar police are simply going to have to get used *to*.

> **Ending a sentence with a preposition is something up with which I will not put.**
>
> **Anonymous**

CHAPTER 2
STUMBLING BLOCKS:
Confusing words

SPOTTING THE DIFFERENCES

The English language is full of confusing pairs and triplets of words that are similar but not identical. In this chapter we're going to look at some of the most common culprits in the field of language mix-ups. Sometimes the meanings of the words are quite distinct, and the problems only arise because we're writing too quickly to really think about the words we're choosing, but in other cases we're presented with two words that sound kind of similar and whose meanings are close enough to make them difficult to choose between. We'll cover both of these kinds of problem here, and we'll also look at one or two straightforward howlers, which you'll need to avoid if you want people to be sure that you know your stuff.

advice **and** *advise*

We'll start off on the beginner slopes, with a pair of words that aren't actually terribly confusing. *Advice* is a noun and *advise* is a verb. When you *advise* somebody, you give them your *advice*. (Often whether they want it or not, in my case.)

advice

- *I took your **advice** and chose this ice-cream flavour.*

- *I'm so glad I listened to his **advice**; the views up here are simply stunning.*

- *As you grow older your **advice** changes.*

advise

- *I'm **advising** you to choose the mint-choc-chip flavour. It's my favourite!*

- *I **advise** you to take the longer route because the views are stunning.*

- *The VR headset can make you forget what's around you, so I **advise** you to clear anything breakable out of the way before you start using it.*

*affect **and** effect*

Aha! Now we're off into slightly more complicated territory. These two words sound exactly the same when most people pronounce them, so it's not surprising that we sometimes mix them up.

Affect is a verb. If you suffer from hay fever, you'll find that every summer the pollen *affects* your eyes and nose. *Effect* is a noun. In the summer, hay-fever sufferers feel the *effects* of the high pollen count.

But it's not all plain sailing with these two words, because, rather confusingly, sometimes *effect* can be a verb. However, it only functions as a verb when it has the meaning 'to bring about a change'. So you'll encounter it in phrases like *The government's new policy is unlikely to effect a positive change on the economy*. This use occurs relatively infrequently, though, so your best guideline is to remember that *affect* is usually used as a verb and *effect* is usually used as a noun. I can promise that this will be an *effective* strategy.

 WHAT NOT TO DO

Causing *alot* of trouble

We're going to keep this one short: *alot* is not a word. If you mean *a lot*, you need two words. If you mean *allot*, as in, to give things to people, you need two *l*s. The cartoonist, writer and blogger Allie Brosh was so incensed by the frequent appearance of the word *alot* on the internet that she created a mythical beast – part bear, part yak and part pug – called an *alot*. With this creature in her mind, sentences such as *I care about this alot* took on a new and grammatically correct (not to mention pleasantly warm and fuzzy) meaning. However, inventing imaginary characters takes a lot (not *alot*) of time and energy, and it would make life easier for Allie and the rest of us if everyone could simply remember that *a lot* is two words! Surely that's not ~~alot~~ *a lot* to ask.

are and *our*

This word pair falls into a category that could be entitled Yes, We Know They're Not the Same Word. *Are* is a verb and *our* is a determiner. The problem is that sometimes when we're typing quickly, the wrong word can slip into *our* texts. So this is simply one to watch out for. Be on your guard! *Our* language is always under attack and you *are* the person who can fix it!

are

- **Are** you going to David's party?

- These paintings **are** fantastic! You should be so proud of yourself.

- **Are** you going to order dessert? The chocolate cake looks so tempting.

our

- I love **our** new home – I can't wait to invite everyone over and have a massive party!

- We took so many photos on **our** holiday in Ibiza.

- **Our** highlight of the holiday was when Lizzie accidently fell into the pool and lost her bikini.

complement **and** *compliment*

Oh, English language, you are so full of words that sound the same while meaning different things! It's as if you were designed to trick us at every turn. Oh well, there's nothing we can do except learn how to decode your secrets and show people we really know our stuff when it comes to your tricky word pairs.

The verb *complement* means to add to or complete something, in a positive way, while the verb *compliment* means to praise somebody for something. If your colleague's new, two-tone bowling shoes *complement* her smart-casual, sports-themed ensemble, you might *compliment* her on her wonderful fashion sense. And if your grammar is *complemented* by a perfect command of the trickiest word pairs in the English language, you are bound to receive a few *compliments* yourself.

complement

- *This filter really **complements** the photo of Jemma standing on the beach last summer.*

- *I would suggest the parsley sauce because it's a nice **complement** to the fish.*

- *I'm going to buy the yellow case as it **complements** my phone.*

compliment

- *They left us **complimentary** mints in our hotel room, but I also took an extra few from the jar in reception.*

- *The service was **complimentary** and they even hoovered the inside of the car!*

- *Why don't you just accept the **compliment**? You look beautiful in that dress.*

desert **and** dessert

These words have very different meanings, but they can test our spelling powers to the limit. Here's an outline of their differences:

desert (noun)	A vast, dry, sandy place – not much fun unless you like that kind of thing and have plenty of water with you.

desert (verb)	To abandon someone or something – again, rarely much fun and sometimes it can get you into serious trouble.
dessert (noun)	Something sweet and delicious that you eat at the end of a meal – lots of fun, especially when it comes in the form of a freakshake that's slightly bigger than your head.

There's no easy way to remember this distinction, except perhaps by remembering that *desserts* are all about exce*ss*, and that double *s* in the middle of *dessert* is far more exce*ss*ive than the dried-up single *s* in *desert*.

After all this talk of deserts and desserts, I find myself suddenly wanting a cold drink and a bowl of nice pavlova…

disinterested **and** *uninterested*

This is one of those differences that gets the language purists all hot and bothered. Such self-appointed experts will be quick to tell you that, while *uninterested* means having no interest in a subject (as in *I am totally uninterested in cricket, because it's so utterly tedious*), *disinterested* means 'impartial' (as in *I am a disinterested observer, and thus perfectly qualified to umpire your cricket match without favouring either of you unfairly*). The truth, however, is that *disinterested* has been used to mean 'uninterested' since the seventeenth century, and more than a quarter of citations in the *Oxford English Dictionary* relate to this sense of the word.

disinterested

- *I'm **disinterested** in this football game as none of my favourite teams are playing.*

- *When my brother and I argue over what we're going to watch on TV, we always ask our mum to decide because she's **disinterested** in the outcome.*

- *I couldn't judge the fancy dress competition because my sister is in it, and they needed a **disinterested** person to choose the winner.*

uninterested

- *I am **uninterested** in him, because he was mean to my friend.*

- *I am **uninterested** in the business course, because maths was always my weakest subject at school.*

- *I am **uninterested** in that trashy TV show.*

Still, it's possible that at your next job interview you might be dealing with a stickler for the 'official' difference between these meanings, so if you choose your words carefully you'll have more chance of receiving a *disinterested* assessment of your suitability for the post than an *uninterested* one.

hear **and** *here*

This is another simple one. *Hear* is the verb that describes perception of sound, and *here* is an adverb of place (specifically, *this* place). But when we're typing quickly, these two homophones (words that sound the same) can be easily mixed up. Especially in sentences such as *I'm in the House of Commons tea room, and I can hear 'hear! hear!' here.*

imply **and** *infer*

These two verbs confound us because they both relate to subtle communication, and they sound rather similar. The difference between them is that *imply* refers to the person doing the communicating, and *infer* refers to the person doing the interpreting.

If I say, shortly before my birthday, *I've seen a really interesting book on grammar in the local bookshop, and I'd love to read it sometime*, I'm *implying* to my partner (who is very long-suffering) that it would be an ideal birthday present for me. He can *infer* from what I've said that I would like to have it as a birthday present. Or, alternatively, he can look pointedly at our bookshelves and say *We do have a lot of books on grammar, don't we?* – leaving me to *infer* that I might have to buy it for myself. Or write my own book on grammar!

infer

• *I hope he **inferred** when I declined his invitation that I already have a date to the prom.*

- *Hopefully my teacher will be able to **infer** from all my hard work that I am intelligent enough to move into the top set.*

- *If I leave the leaflet on the kitchen side, Mum will **infer** that I really want to go on the school trip.*

imply

- *I have **implied** that I'm brave enough to go on the ghost train by going on the rollercoaster.*

- *When Abbie and I went to the shop, I **implied** that the red pair of shoes were my favourite.*

- *Chris didn't have to say anything: his body language **implied** very clearly that he was annoyed with me.*

know, *no* **and** *now*

These three words are very different, and only two of them sound the same, but they have a habit of creeping into my typing, so I thought I should outline them here.

To *know* is to be aware of something; *no* is, among other things, the word we use to decline and refuse things; and *now* is the present moment. But even though these differences are easy to define, when we're faced with sentences like *I knew it then, but I don't know it now, no*, unless you're concentrating, it's easy to type something that's a plain *no-no*.

know

- *I am going to share everything I **know** with him, because he is my best friend.*

- *I **know** for a fact that you and I shall be friends forever.*

- *Martin is very intelligent; he **knows** a lot about the subject he is studying.*

no

- *Sorry, I can't make it tonight. Mum said **no** – apparently the film is too gory.*

- ***No**, thank you, I don't want a loyalty card as I don't come here often.*

- *I have **no** idea when my selfie stick will arrive, but I hope it comes before we go away.*

now

- *I couldn't possibly tell you how I'm feeling right **now**.*

- *It was hilarious looking at old photos and comparing them to what we look like **now**.*

- *I realise **now** that I've made a massive mistake.*

 WHAT NOT TO DO

Making *literally* the worst mistake of your life

Literally is possibly one of the most abused words in the English language. If something *literally* happened, then it did actually happen. If it only happened in a metaphorical sense, then it's not *literal* but *figurative*.

This means that if you say *When the teacher saw the mess I'd made, she literally exploded*, you mean that she actually, in real life, blew into hundreds of pieces, creating a bigger mess than the one that had angered her. This rarely happens, and generally when somebody says *she literally exploded*, it's safe to assume that she *figuratively exploded* or she *literally shouted a lot and went red in the face*.

In formal speech or writing it's best to use the word *literally* only in its literal sense, but its figurative use goes back to the beginning of the twentieth century, so this is probably a linguistic issue where we'll need to stop trying to hold back the tide eventually. If the abuse of the word *literally* is making you *literally* see red, it's probably best if you relax a little and remember that sometimes a descriptive approach to the English language makes life easier for everyone. Literally.

loose and *lose*

This is another pair of words whose meanings are quite different, but whose spellings lead us into error from time to time. *Loose* is an adjective describing a thing that is not tight, while *lose* is a verb meaning to fail to keep something. If the straps that attach your suitcases to the roof rack of your car are too *loose*, you may *lose* your luggage before you reach your holiday destination. At which point, tongues will become *looser*, and tempers will be *lost* along with your beach shorts and bucket and spade set. Far better to keep these words in their correct places and ensure that sandcastles are built by happy holidaymakers!

loose

- *My jeans were much **looser** before Christmas – that's because Santa brought me so much chocolate this year.*

- *That screw looks a little **loose** so you might want to check it out.*

- *Oh no – my wristband has fallen off! It must have been too **loose** on my wrist.*

lose

- *If I don't get my ring resized soon I know that I will end up **losing** it.*

- *I somehow managed to **lose** my phone when I was out last night.*

- *We always have to be careful not to **lose** my little brother. He always runs off when we have our backs turned.*

pore over **and** pour over

We'll just focus for now on the verb definitions of these words, and not get distracted by the *pores* on our skin. If you *pore over* something, you read or study it in close detail. It's probably fair to say that a good beauty therapist will *pore over* your pores when they give you a facial. Contrastingly, *pour over* means to release something that flows in a steady stream over something else. When you stand in the shower, water *pours over* your head, and on a hot day, you *pour* water *over* the flowers. Equally, the beauty therapist, having finished *poring over* your pores, might *pour* some replenishing (and no doubt very expensive) oil *over* your face, sending you out into the world more beautiful than ever, and more self-assuredly expert in your grip on English grammar.

pore

- *I need to **pore** over these notes so I'm ready for my exam tomorrow.*

- *I can't wait to **pore** over my new graphic art book; the subject is so fascinating.*

- *Gemma always spending hours **poring** through clothes catalogues to choose her perfect look for the season.*

pour

- *I can't wait to **pour** this chocolate sauce all over my ice cream.*

- *Could you **pour** a little more milk in my coffee please? It's a tad strong.*

- *I'm going to **pour** this warm water over the dog because he's filthy!*

practice **and** practise

These two words sound exactly the same, so it's no wonder we don't always know which to choose. In British English, *practice* is a noun and *practise* is a verb. When you *practise* the piano, you are doing your piano *practice*. The easiest way to remember this difference is by comparing the two words to the words *advice* (noun) and *advise* (verb). Because these two words are pronounced differently, it's easy to remember how to tell them apart and then apply this rule to the words *practice* and *practise*.

In American English, you don't need to work nearly as hard to remember the difference between these two spellings, as Americans use the spelling *practice* for both the noun and the verb. It's as if they found some of the quirks of the Old World's language *practices* to be unhelpfully confusing, and wanted to improve things for everyone on their side of the Atlantic. Oh.

practice

- *Instead of chatting about it, perhaps it would be better to put into* **practice**.

- *The doctor's I go to on a regular basis is a private* **practice**.

- *He turned up to choir* **practice** *late.*

practise

- I will be down for dinner in a moment; I'm just **practising** some killer dance moves.

- I was rubbish at shooting before I started **practising** my penalty kicks.

- I saw the athletes **practising** for the Olympics at the weekend – it was amazing!

principal **and** *principle*

This is another word pair that sounds exactly the same, and I have to confess I always have to scurry up into my mental language-reference loft before I take the risk of spelling one of them. So let's lay it out here:

A *principle* is an abstract noun meaning a strongly held belief that guides your behaviour, or a fundamental quality of something. If you are *principled*, you are morally upright and good.

Principal is an adjective describing the main or most important thing or the most important quality of a thing. Water is the *principal* ingredient of tea, and tea is the *principal* fuel that keeps Britain moving. A *principal*, by extension, can be the most important person in an organisation, particularly in a school or other educational institution.

If you are good at sticking to the *principal principles* of your school or college, then you probably won't be one of the *principal* offenders called up to see the *Principal*. Which is one of the *principal* benefits of having *principles*!

 WHAT NOT TO DO

Talking pacifically

When I first heard this linguistic car crash playing out in front of me, I thought my ears were at fault, but it has continued to play itself out in the soundtrack of my life, and my ears appear to be working as well as ever. What was this baffling quirk, you ask? It was somebody using the word *pacifically* instead of the (appropriate) word *specifically*. Now, this is a usage that needs to go the same way as the *alot*, which appeared at the start of this chapter. It needs to stop! And you definitely need to avoid this mistake if you want people to know that you know your stuff about the English language. Let's stop for a moment (so I can take a few deep, calming breaths) and look at these two words.

The adjective *pacific* means 'peaceful'. The adjective *specific* means 'clearly identified'. If you say *Let's look at this one pacifically*, you are saying that we all need to chill out, calm down and look at this in a peaceful manner. However, I would place a *lot* of money – in fact, my entire life savings (which is not actually a lot of money, truth be told) – on the bet that what you actually meant was *Let's look at this one specifically*, or *Let's look at this one, not the whole lot*.

The sooner people stop saying *pacifically* when they mean *specifically*, the more *pacifically* grammar pedants like me will start viewing the rest of humanity. And *specifically* the people who have now stopped abusing the word *pacifically*.

to, two and too

Like *hear* and *here*, these words are not confusing in their meanings – it's simply the fact that they all sound the same that can lead to mix-ups on the page.

to	A preposition expressing movement in the direction of a particular place.
two	A number particularly suited for tea and tangoing, though not at the same time.
too	An adverb conveying the concept of excess: *I have had too much tea to tango.*

to

- *I'm going **to** the shops; does anybody want anything?*

- *It's fairly easy **to** go from Brighton **to** London; the train journey takes just under an hour.*

- *It has taken a lot of hard work **to** get **to** where I am now.*

too

- *I have **too** many watches for someone who is always late!*

- *This colour is **too** bright; I think the dark green would suit your complexion more.*

- *Don't overdo it **too** much or you will end up hurting yourself.*

two

- *This photo is so cute! You look like **two** peas in a pod.*

- *You know what they say: **two** minds are always better than one.*

- *My teacher made me stay after school **two** days in a row when she caught me using Snapchat in class.*

try and **and** *try to*

I can hear the grammar police's helicopter circling overhead as we approach the thorny issue of *try and* vs *try to*. In everyday conversation, it's quite common to use the formation *try and*, in sentences such as *I haven't got time to talk now, but I'll try and call you later*. Grammar guardians decry this usage because it's not strictly watertight: for example, you can't use it in other tenses (*I am trying and call him now* and *I tried and call you but your phone was switched off* both sound odd and don't make sense). They would advocate the grammatically sound reworking of this sentence instead: *I haven't got time to talk now, but I'll try to call you later*.

The best guidance here is to accept the usage of *try and* in everyday conversations and informal writing, but to avoid it in favour of the more accurate formation *try to* in any context where correctness and formality will be appreciated.

weather and *whether*

This is another sneaky sound-alike pair waiting to slip under the radar of your spellcheck and trip you up. The *weather* outside may be frightful, but *whether* it's frightful or not, we can still have a lovely time indoors reading about grammar. I think that's all we need to say about this one!

weather

- *If the **weather** is nice, I really want to go camping this weekend.*

- *If I'm honest, my dream job would be working as a **weather** forecaster on TV.*

- *People in England are always complaining about the **weather**; it's a part of the culture!*

whether

- *I don't know **whether** she would mind if I borrowed her phone.*

- *I'm going to ask my teacher **whether** it's better to study this in the morning or in the evening.*

- *Someone told me that it's cheaper if you buy the whole package, but I don't know **whether** he just made it up.*

WHAT NOT TO DO

Would have vs would of

What a great way to end this chapter, with another clang of the great grammar gong and a stark warning about another grammatical sin to avoid. When we use conditional forms, particularly in speech, we often crush the helpful auxiliary verb *have* into a tiny sound: sentences like *We would have won if the other team hadn't scored* are often shortened to *We would've won if the other team hadn't scored*. This leads some people to deduce that *would've* is actually a contraction of *would of*, and this means that *would of*, *could of* and *should of* appear more often than they should in written texts.

If you want your language to impress, using *have* in conditional clauses will ensure you have no regrets. Whether you get the job or not, you'll know there's nothing you *could have* expressed more accurately in your application. (And they obviously *should have* given you the job, with excellent grammar like yours.)

> ❝ *In any language it is a struggle to make a sentence say exactly what you mean.* ❞
> Arthur Koestler

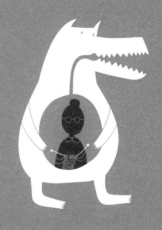

CHAPTER 3
DOTS AND DASHES:
Punctuation

PERFECTING YOUR PUNCTUATION

Now that we've looked at words and all the forms they come in, it's time to turn our attention to those little black dots and dashes that are sprinkled throughout any text. Most of us feel pretty good about full stops and question marks, but even the brainiest and smartest among us can feel a bit unnerved by a semicolon. But never fear, in this chapter we'll be looking at each mark in detail, and by the end you'll be a black belt in the Dark Arts of Punctuation.

> ❝ *Write one good clean sentence and put a period at the end of it. Then write another one.* ❞
>
> M. F. K. Fisher

FULL STOP .

Also known as a 'period' in US English, this handy little dot tells us we've reached the end of a sentence.

I love learning all about grammar.

Full stops are also used to indicate abbreviated (shortened) words:

I was born on 30 Dec. 1995.

Here are a few common abbreviations you'll see in books and other texts:

Co.	*Company*
etc.	*et cetera*
e.g.	*exempli gratia*
St.	*Street*

A comprehensive list of abbreviations can be found in Appendix 2 at the back of the book.

THINKING OUTSIDE THE BOX

Punctuation innovators

Not everyone uses punctuation marks in the ways that are commonly taught and accepted. For example, in the last chapter of his groundbreaking novel *Ulysses*, James Joyce wrote eight long 'sentences', one of them reaching a length of 4,391 words, to reveal his character Molly Bloom's stream of consciousness, and the whole chapter contains only two full stops. At an opposite extreme, Eimear McBride's award-winning novel *A Girl Is a Half-formed Thing*, published in 2013, challenges the reader with its torrent of (literally) half-formed sentences. Still, if you are writing with the aim of making your text easy to understand, it's probably wisest to follow the standard practices of punctuation. Rule-breaking often works best in highly literary contexts, where it is acceptable to ask the reader to give their full attention to interpreting the text.

COMMA ,

You can stop for a proper breather after a full stop, but after a comma you just get a little break, long enough to gather your wits for the next part of the sentence. These curly symbols have lots of different uses in our text, as we'll see below.

(1) Commas are used to separate items in lists, like this:

I love learning about grammar, spelling and porcupine rodeos.

Note that in British English we don't usually insert a comma before the word *and* in lists such as the one above. In American English (and certain British publishers' house styles), a comma appears before the *and*:

I love learning about grammar, spelling, and porcupine rodeos.

This bonus comma is known as the 'serial comma', the 'Oxford comma' or the 'Harvard comma', and it is the subject of a surprisingly large amount of debate among grammar lovers. (Always a good icebreaker at parties. Or it would be if grammar lovers went to parties.)

Sometimes, even in styles that don't favour the serial comma, its use can help to remove ambiguity in lists that have multi-word items. This sentence is a little unclear in its current phrasing:

> *Today's specials are steak and kidney pie, bangers and mash and cheese and tomato quiche.*

Is the second item *bangers and mash*, followed by *cheese and tomato quiche*, or is it a plain plate of *bangers*, followed by *mash and cheese and tomato quiche*? Anyone who has a passing acquaintance with classic pub grub would guess at the first of these two possibilities, but in unfamiliar contexts, lists lacking a serial comma could lead to genuine confusion. In cases such as these, a serial comma can help to make one's food options clear from the first perusal of the pub menu:

Today's specials are steak and kidney pie, bangers and mash, and cheese and tomato quiche.

(2) Commas are used to separate clauses in a sentence:

As I had forgotten my saddle, I knew the porcupine rodeo was really going to hurt this time.

(3) Commas are also used before and after quoted speech:

Robert strode merrily down the hall, calling over his shoulder, 'I'll be back later – wish me luck in the Golden Spines Derby!'

'You care about those porcupines more than you care about me,' Amanda complained to herself, as the door closed with a bang.

(4) Finally, commas can be used to help mark off part of a sentence, so we know which bit is which:

My porcupine, Marvin, was looking especially grumpy that morning. I feared that this rodeo, like so many others, would not end well.

> **" Part of the beauty of a comma is that it offers a rest… It allows us to catch our breath. "**
> Pico Iyer

✕ WHAT NOT TO DO

Comma confusion

Sometimes a misplaced or missing comma can be the difference between normality and disaster.

what they said	what they meant to say
Let's eat Grandma! (Was there an outbreak of cannibalism in the family?)	*Let's eat, Grandma!*
I like cooking my family and my pets. (More cannibalism?)	*I like cooking, my family and my pets.*
Stop clubbing, baby seals. (You crazy young seal pups. You need to go to bed early!)	*Stop clubbing baby seals.*
I'm sorry I love you. (I wish I didn't love you.)	*I'm sorry, I love you.*

ELLIPSIS ...

Don't worry, 'ellipsis' is just the fancy name for those three little dots in a row that you often see in texts. Ellipses have two main uses:

(1) Ellipses can be used in quoted text to indicate that something has been left out. Imagine that your band's latest gig receives a review like this:

Suburban Dirtbag showed their total lack of class in a performance that was, sadly, unforgettable.

You might want to quote this praise on your next album cover with a couple of well-placed ellipses:

Suburban Dirtbag showed their total... class in a performance that was... unforgettable.

(2) Ellipses are sometimes used to show that something has been left unsaid, or that the writer or speaker has paused or tailed off without finishing their thought.

'Darling, for your birthday I've bought us two tickets to the next Suburban Dirtbag concert!'

'Oh, goodness... That's so incredibly... thoughtful of you.'

This second way of using an ellipsis occurs a lot in personal emails and other kinds of informal writing. It's best to avoid these 'unfinished thoughts' ellipses in formal writing such as a business report or school essay, unless you're sure they're appropriate.

COLON :

Yes, it's a part of the body that we try to keep quiet in polite company, but it's also a very useful punctuation mark. Life's funny like that. The colon has one main purpose, and it's very easy to grasp. These two little dots are used to separate a more general thought, which comes first, from a more specific example or explanation, which follows it.

The part before the colon is usually a complete sentence, but the part after it doesn't need to be: it can be a single word, a whole sentence or a list of items. (Did you see what I did there?) So, here are a few examples of colons in action:

You'll never believe what Mark gave me for my birthday: tickets to see Suburban Dirtbag!

There are three things I can't stand: punk rock, going to gigs and Mark buying me presents that he really wants for himself.

I saw Susan last week and she told me she'd had a life-changing experience: she went to see Suburban Dirtbag with Mark, and now she wants to be a punk rocker.

• • •

Firstly, I will explain my goal: I want to be a successful painter because I'm passionate about art.

Being an art student is a lot of hard work: motivation, perseverance and creativity are all essential factors if you are going to do well.

SEMICOLON ;

This is probably the most feared weapon in the writer's armoury: if you can use a semicolon with confidence, you are essentially showing the world you're at the top of your punctuation game.

However, we don't actually need to get too technical about the semicolon. Its main use is to join two complete sentences that balance each other but don't really work as separate sentences. Another way of thinking of the semicolon is that it's a break between two ideas that's longer than a comma and shorter than a full stop. You have time to breathe, but you don't want to let the first idea drop completely before you start the second one.

I always used to hate punk music; now I know it's the sound of my brain catching fire, and I can't get enough of it.

• • •

Art is so important to me; it's a part of everyday life.

A second use of the semicolon is to separate items in lists, particularly when the list is preceded by a colon or when the listed elements contain commas.

Next summer I'm planning a tour of punk's great landmark venues: The Brighton Bar in Long Branch, New Jersey; SO36 in Kreuzberg, Berlin; and The Fat Ferret in Portsmouth, Hampshire.

* * *

There are three main places I want to visit for my art project: Barcelona, for the Sagrada Familia; the Picasso exhibition in Bruges; and Paris, to see the Venus de Milo in the Louvre museum.

QUESTION MARK ?

This symbol won't hold us up for long; a question mark is used at the end of a sentence to tell the reader that it is a question.

Why are there so many punctuation marks?

If I decide to wear this dress, will I be warm enough?

When you go bungee jumping do you feel sick afterwards?

Are you from this part of the country?

In quoted speech, questions end with a question mark, even if the whole sentence needs to end with a full stop.

'Why are there so many punctuation marks?' Amanda asked.

'If I decide to wear this dress, will I be warm enough?' Josie wondered to herself.

'When you go bungee jumping do you feel sick afterwards?' Johnny asked nervously.

'Are you from this part of the country?' Billie enquired.

But if the speech is being quoted indirectly, no question mark is needed.

Amanda asked why there were so many punctuation marks. I told her I had no idea.

Josie wondered if she would be warm enough if she wore that dress.

Johnny asked nervously if Peter felt sick after he went bungee jumping.

Billie enquired if Shirley was from this part of the country.

EXCLAMATION MARK !

This is another simple one, and the most fun to write: nobody can feel totally neutral ending a sentence with this lightning strike of a mark. It's used at the end of a sentence – which can be very short – to show strong emotion. Here are a few examples of writing losing its cool:

Help!

Oh my God, Sophie's computer is on fire!

You'll never believe it: Sophie typed so fast she set her computer on fire today!

•••

This tastes seriously scrumptious!

This chocolate cake melts in your mouth – the taste is unbelievable!

I am so embarrassed but it was totally worth it; I can't believe I ate an entire chocolate cake this afternoon!

As you can see, exclamation marks do get a bit wearing after a while, and it's best not to use too many of them. In formal writing they're best avoided, and you should never *ever* use two or more in a row, unless you're messaging someone, in which case most of the rules of grammar and punctuation go out of the window anyway.

> **“ Cut out all these exclamation points. An exclamation point is like laughing at your own joke. ”**
> F. Scott Fitzgerald

QUOTATION MARKS ‘ ’ “ ”

These are used to indicate speech, and they come in two types: single quotes ‘ ’ and double quotes “ ”. It doesn't really matter which type you use, as long as you use them consistently. Americans tend to prefer double quotes, while the British are more likely to use single quotes.

The only slightly tricky thing about quoted speech is knowing how to join the spoken bit to the explanation of who is speaking. If the introductory bit comes *first*, you need a comma before the spoken words, like this:

> Harry cleared his throat and said, 'The food is running out – we only have three days' supply left in the boat.'

If the explanation of who is speaking comes *after* a spoken sentence, the spoken words end with a comma:

> 'If only you'd told us sooner,' the captain replied with a sigh.

Question marks and exclamation marks work in exactly the same way in quoted speech:

> 'Does it make any difference?' Harry asked, starting to look around the cabin rather nervously.

> 'Yes, we would have eaten you last week, while you were still fat and juicy!' snapped the captain, reaching for his pistol.

Quotation marks are also used to show that a word or phrase has been quoted directly from another source, which can be a useful way of showing that the quoted words are not your own work or your own opinion:

> *The captain served a casserole that evening made of a meat he described as 'somewhat like chicken'. Harry didn't join them for the meal, which the crew thought was strange.*

Finally, the two styles of quotation marks come into play in the same sentence when a person is speaking and quotes another person as they do so:

> *'Don't worry,' said the captain. 'I saw Harry this afternoon and he said, "I really want to finish watching the extended edition of The Hobbit on my laptop – you go ahead and eat without me."'*

PARENTHESES ( ) [ ]

Parentheses, also known as brackets, always come in pairs, and perform the function of separating off information that is relevant, but not essential, to the main content of a sentence.

They can occur within a sentence, or in a sentence of their own:

John admitted (rather reluctantly) that my risotto tasted as good as if a real Italian chef had made it. (I didn't tell him that I'd ordered it from Bistro Pronto and reheated it just before John arrived.)

Square brackets [ ] pop up occasionally in written English, usually to indicate a relevant piece of information that was not given in an extract of quoted material:

The director of the production said, 'We never mention the name of the Scottish play [Macbeth] in front of the actors. You can't be too careful.'

One important detail that will put you firmly in the best-brackets bracket is how you place punctuation in and around parenthetical phrases and sentences.

The key is to remember that any punctuation that belongs to the main sentence, rather than the bracketed words, should stay outside the brackets. The main sentence should still make sense if you were to remove the section in parentheses, as in the following example:

I didn't want to comment on Chris's new shorts (because you don't criticise the boss, and these were hideous), so I pretended I'd lost my voice for the rest of the office party.

However, if the brackets are enclosing an entire sentence, the closing punctuation needs to be inside the closing bracket:

(I made a mental note to contract malaria before next year's party so I wouldn't have to go.)

APOSTROPHE '

If the semicolon is the sign of punctuation mastery, misuse of apostrophes is probably the klaxon of punctuation chaos. People love apostrophes, but sometimes it seems as if we use them randomly: throw in a couple of apostrophes, shake the sentence around until they stick and everything will be fine. Well, listen up! There are only two main ways to use apostrophes, and when you have them firmly under your belt, you will feel a pure and rapturous smugness that will make you thoroughly annoying to all your friends. And that *has* to be a good thing.

(1) Apostrophes are used to show possession.

You must never ever go into Kevin's bedroom on the night of a full moon.

If the thing doing the possessing is singular (like *Kevin*), the apostrophe comes *before* the *s*. However, for plural nouns that end with an *s*, the apostrophe comes *after* the *s*:

Kevin Henderson invited me to sleep over last week, but my parents say there's something funny about the Hendersons' house.

If a plural noun doesn't end with an *s*, then the apostrophe comes before the *s*, not after it:

> Kevin told me he prefers werewolf movies to children's movies every time.

Getting this right marks you out as a punctuation pro.

Finally, if a person's name ends with an *s*, we generally add *'s* to the end of the name if you would pronounce it with an extra '*s*' sound on the end, but just an apostrophe (without an extra *s*) if you wouldn't. So, for example:

> Jess's horse
> Charles's pterodactyl
> Beau Bridges' page on Wikipedia
> Bridget Jones's Diary
> Augustus's glasses were foggy
> Ellis's heart was racing

(2) Apostrophes are used to show contractions, or letters that have been missed out of a word.

Contractions occur most often in spoken English, but they're also used increasingly frequently in all but the most formal documents. Here are some common examples:

I am	I'm	has not	hasn't
he is	he's	does not	doesn't
she is	she's		

As well as being used for these widely accepted and commonly used contractions, apostrophes are also used to indicate letters that are dropped in colloquial speech. For example, a person's speech might be accurately written as:

What you doin' round 'ere again? Olly said 'e'll thump you next time 'e sees you.

This might be more true to life than the more fully written out version:

What are you doing round here again? Olly said he'll thump you next time he sees you.

PROBLEM SOLVER

Avoiding apostrophe confusion

It's very easy to mix up possession and contraction, and to insert apostrophes where they don't belong. This is especially common when a word exists in two forms: one with an apostrophe and one without an apostrophe. Here are some hidden-in-plain-sight traps to watch out for.

its and *it's*

its is the possessive form of *it*:	*it's* is the contracted form of *it is*:
I'm not touching that porcupine! **Its** spines are way too prickly.	I'm not touching that porcupine! **It's** covered in prickly spines.
I love this book. **Its** cover is so beautiful.	I love this cover. **It's** so beautiful.

there, their and they're

there is an adverb used to describe a place or position:	their is the possessive form of they:	they're is the contracted form of they are:
I was beamed into an alien spacecraft yesterday and I had a really great time **there**. It was over **there** where we first said hello to each other.	The aliens told me **their** home planet doesn't have any televisions or mobile phones. You could tell by **their** incessant conversation that they would be friends forever.	**They're** going to move here permanently because they love watching **The X Factor** and putting selfies on Instagram. Even after all the ups and down, **they're** still best friends.

whose **and** *who's*

whose **is used to define something belonging to or associated with a person:**	*who's* **is the contracted form of** *who is* **or** *who has***:**
I don't know **whose** *milk was in the fridge, but I needed it for my cereal this morning.* **Whose** *car are we going in to the cinema tonight?*	**Who's** *[who is] the one who drank my milk and didn't replace it?* **Who's** *[who has] been drinking my milk? I've had enough of this!* **Who's** *up for coming to the cinema tonight?*

your and *you're*

your is the possessive form of *you*:	*you're* is the contracted form of *you are*:
Your taste in karaoke music is remarkable. *Your* music and fashion tastes are quite eccentric.	*You're* one of the worst karaoke singers I have ever heard. *You're* quite an eccentric person.

Crimes against apostrophes are all too common, and if you really want to hurt a grammar purist, try sending them a message saying, 'I think your great.' But if you simply want to communicate clearly and effectively, use these words correctly and show the world you really know your stuff..

WHAT NOT TO DO

Apostrophes that need to be abolished

Some words don't need apostrophes but attract them nonetheless, just as any opinion expressed on the internet attracts poorly punctuated abusive comments. There's something about the jaunty little flick of an apostrophe that makes us yearn to insert them in words that should be unadorned. These words tend to be plurals of nouns whose singular forms end with a vowel: there's a deep-seated longing in many of us to somehow 'improve' these plurals with an apostrophe. However, if you remember the golden rule – that apostrophes exist to show possession or contraction – you can avoid the siren song of the 'greengrocer's apostrophe'.

wrong	right
banana's	*bananas*

ladie's	ladies
no dog's allowed	no dogs allowed
panini's	paninis
special deal's	special deals

There are apostrophe activists who go around eliminating these apostrophes wherever they can and pointing them out in a smug voice to their friends. You do not need to become such a person. Simply knowing that you are an apostrophe expert will enable you to sail through life with a smile on *you're* face. I mean, with a smile on *your* face. Phew.

HYPHEN -

Hyphens are less fashionable than they used to be, but they are still important in helping us to express ourselves clearly when we write. They have three main uses:

(1) Creating compound words.

Sometimes the addition of a hyphen can clarify the exact meaning of a phrase. The newspaper headline *Bird-eating spider found in banana crate* has a different meaning from *Bird eating spider found in banana crate*.

Opinions differ on which compound words and phrases require hyphens. Different sources will offer the spellings *bootcamp*, *boot camp* and *boot-camp*. The best course of action is to choose one main reference source, such as one of the standard dictionaries, and follow its guidance.

(2) Connecting prefixes to words.

Hyphens can be used to join prefixes such as *co-*, *pre-* and *re-* to words, particularly when the word would be hard to decipher without a hyphen, such as *de-ice* instead of *deice*, or *pre-exist* instead of *preexist*. This is another area of language where different sources will give different advice, and again, the best advice is to follow the guidance of one good dictionary, to ensure that your use of hyphens is consistent.

(3) Breaking words at the end of a line.

Thanks to computers, we rarely have to worry about how much space we have at the end of a line, and whether the final word will fit into the remaining space or have to be chopped into two pieces with a hyphen. However, it does happen occasionally, and you'll often see hyphenated word breaks in books and newspapers, especially when space is at a premium.

If you need to break a word in two with a hyphen, you need to think about its component parts, and, if possible, insert the hyphen between two of them.

For example, *dis-appearance* and *disappear-ance* make more sense than *disa-ppearance* and *disappea-rance*. For advice on where to insert hyphens, the best place to turn to is a spelling dictionary, such as the *New Oxford Spelling Dictionary* (see Further Reading for details).

DASH – —

Some punctuation perfectionists pooh-pooh the dash as being not quite correct enough – sentences involving dashes have a certain impetuousness to them which bothers the more strait-laced among us. But don't worry – dashes are here to stay, and you are allowed to use them in all but the most formal of writing.

Dashes come in two sizes. An **em dash** looks like this — and it gets its name because an em is a unit of measurement generally equivalent to the width of a capital M in most fonts, and the dash has exactly this width. An **en dash** looks like this – and its name is derived from the fact that it tends to have the same width as the letter N in any given font, although in some fonts an en dash is simply half the width of an em dash.

Different styles prefer one dash over the other, so you can follow the advice of your chosen dictionary or style guide. In general, British English tends to prefer en dashes while American English favours em dashes, but it's not a hard and fast rule. The one point to note is that en dashes tend to have spaces around them – like this – while em dashes are generally joined up—like this.

The simplest way to think about dashes is to consider where you would naturally insert a pause in a sentence. So, for example, you might find a dash in these places:

On both ends of a parenthetical aside:

I was staying in my parents' summer house – a creaky old cabin deep in the forest – for the summer.

After being told he wasn't allowed out – his mum was angry that he hadn't attended the Villager of the

Year award ceremony – he still managed to sneak out of his bedroom window and meet his friends.

Before an explanation:

I was all alone – Kerry had just broken up with me, but I wasn't about to miss out on my summer break just because he wouldn't be there to enjoy it with me.

The dress was fine until she got her hands on it – now it looks like something my Grandma would wear to a Halloween party.

Before a surprising twist or paradoxical counter-statement:

I looked out of the window and saw something I could never have imagined – a ragged troupe of zombies staggering up the path towards the cabin.

It was so funny – she missed the chair and landed straight on her bum!

Separating a list from the rest of a sentence:

Luckily, I had everything I needed – grenades, a machine gun and a plentiful supply of ammo – so I sat back and waited for Zombiegeddon to begin.

You have access to everything with this ticket – facials, a hot-stone massage, the swimming pool and the sauna – and you can use it twice!

SO, WHY SHOULD I CARE ABOUT PUNCTUATION?

We've looked at a lot of rules and examples in this chapter, and it may all seem a bit academic and dusty. However, the following example will show you just how important punctuation can be. When you put the dots and dashes in different places, the meaning of a sentence can be turned on its head.

A woman, without her man, is nothing.

A woman: without her, man is nothing.

With the right punctuation, you'll be able to say what you mean, and your sentences will be successes.

> **Style is a very simple matter; it is all rhythm. Once you get that, you can't use the wrong words.**
> Virginia Woolf

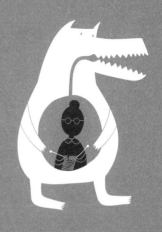

CONCLUSION
REALLY KNOWING YOUR STUFF

THE FINAL FRONTIER

“ *By writing much, one learns to write well.* **”**
Robert Southey

We've looked at a lot (not *alot*) of grammar, vocabulary and punctuation, and whether you've read the whole book from cover to cover or dipped into individual sections, I hope you've found it useful.

As I mentioned at the beginning, some people are happy to watch language usage changing around them and to swim with the tide to keep up, while others defend the old ways against the new, building sea defences to try to stop the new ways from encroaching on the good, solid, dry land of language as we know it today.

In language use, as in many things, it's probably best to choose a middle path. On the one hand, if you go out of your way to learn every grammar rule, and then attempt to apply it to everything that you say or write, you'll quickly discover that (whisper it) *nobody actually agrees on what all the rules are!* Even the standard reference works reach different conclusions on some language issues, and house style documents used by publishers also vary greatly in their pronouncements. On the other hand, if you take a completely easy-going approach to your speaking and writing, you may find yourself using words and phrases in ways that are inappropriate for the context you're in: the wrong word at the wrong time can be at best baffling and at worst offensive.

The secret is to know your audience and to choose a style of speaking or writing that works for them. Here are some examples to show how our choice of words changes depending on the context we're writing for:

Text message to a friend:

hey that BBQ was amazing lol – never thought Paul and Fiona would get together like that OMG. cu monday j xxx

Text message to a colleague:

Hi there Paul, I think you left your hat in my garden after the BBQ – I'll bring it in on Monday. All the best, J

Email to a team of colleagues:

Hi everyone,

This is just to let you know that the next staff barbecue will be held at Thistleton Park on 23 July 2016. Burgers, vegetarian options and buns will be supplied, but we hope you can bring salads and desserts. Here is a link to a spreadsheet on the server so you can fill in the food you're bringing.

Thanks, everyone! I'm looking forward to seeing you at the barbecue.

Jane

Email applying for a job:

Dear Ms Green,

In response to your advertisement in The Warblington Courier, I am writing to apply for the position of Chief Barbecue Officer at Barford International.

I have considerable experience in the field of outdoor cookery and recently organised a barbecue for 60 members of staff in my current firm. I am keen to develop my barbecuing skills and take on the challenge of organising events for a larger group of colleagues, and I feel that my values are very closely aligned with those of Barford International.

I am attaching my CV, which gives further details about my background and skills. If you have any questions, please do not hesitate to contact me.

I hope that my application is of interest and I look forward to hearing from you.

Yours sincerely,
Jane Stallard

When you're writing to your friends, especially on a device with a small screen and a smaller keyboard, it's perfectly acceptable to break the rules of spelling and punctuation: as long as you and your friends understand each other, that's all that matters.

When you're writing in a slightly more formal situation, such as a friendly text message to a colleague you know reasonably well, your language use will probably neaten up a bit.

In a work context, the language becomes more formal and possibly a little more impersonal – it's work, and you need to convey a professional image to your colleagues, particularly in a group email about a serious subject.

Finally, an email accompanying a job application will be one of the most formal messages you will ever write. You will spend time thinking about how you can give the reader the very best impression of yourself, and you will use serious, non-slangy words to express your thoughts. Before you hit 'send', you will read and re-read the email (and maybe even ask a friend to read it for you with fresh eyes), because it's so important to make it as close to perfect as possible. That job as Chief Barbecue Officer could be yours – but only if you start with a cast-iron application.

We can conclude from this that there is not one perfect way to write in English – there are, in fact, several. There's a jokey, flexible way, a careful, accurate way and everything in between. My aim with this book has been to help you decode some of the mysteries of the English language and to understand how its machinery works. With this understanding, you'll be able to choose the best words every time – and people who read your writing will know, without a sliver of doubt, that you are somebody who really knows their stuff.

> **" Write for the most intelligent, wittiest, wisest audience in the universe: write to please yourself. "**
> Harlan Ellison

TEST YOURSELF!

Now's the chance to check if you know your stuff when it comes to grammar. Good luck!

Less and fewer

Fill in the correct word (*less* or *fewer*) before each of the following:

1 .... mistakes
2 .... time
3 .... people
4 .... happiness
5 .... water
6 .... cats
7 .... hair
8 .... hairs
9 .... bottles
10 .... lemonade

Adjectives and adverbs

Choose the word that fits best in each of the following sentences:

1   I'm not going with Paul because he drives
    ....
    (terrible/terribly)

2   Lions are .... animals and don't make
    great pets.
    (wild/wildly)

3   Abi's cakes are always ....
    (delicious/deliciously)

4   Sophie trained .... for the triathlon.
    (rigorous/rigorously)

5   The teacher smiled .... at the students,
    hoping one of them would know the answer.
    (kind/kindly)

6   I'll ask Amanda to sing at my wedding because
    she has a really .... voice.
    (good/well)

7   He walked .... off the stage, thinking already of next year's *X Factor* auditions.
    (*slow*/*slowly*)

8   My phone rang .... in the middle of the silent exam room.
    (*loud*/*loudly*)

9   He plays hockey so .... , I think he should try for the national squad.
    (*good*/*well*)

10 The party was so .... that it kept me awake all night.
    (*raucous*/*raucously*)

Apostrophes in contractions

In each of the following sentences, choose the correct word from the options given.

1   *Its*/*It's* a beautiful day today.

2 *Your/You're* hair looks ridiculous! Why did you dye it pink?

3 Chris gave me a single red rose on Valentine's Day, but *its/it's* thorns stuck in my hand and made it bleed.

4 Fiona and Paul phoned me just now to say *their/they're* running late.

5 *Their/There* babysitter let them down again.

6 I dropped my phone down the loo and now *it's/its* not working.

7 *Whos/Who's* going to Emily's party on Saturday?

8 I don't know *whose/who's* coat that is.

9 Is *there/they're* a label on it?

10 *Your/You're* driving me crazy with all these grammar questions!

Possessive apostrophes

For each of the following examples, which of the given options is correct? Be careful: in some cases, *both* answers might be correct, depending on the context.

1   The .... ball went over the wall and the neighbour wouldn't give it back.
    (a) *boy's*
    (b) *boys'*

2   The .... teacher said she would keep them after school if they didn't behave themselves.
    (a) *children's*
    (b) *childrens'*

3   .... hair is so sleek and shiny – I wish mine looked like that.
    (a) *Liam's*
    (b) *Liams'*

4 I'm sorry, we've completely sold out of ....
Would you like a wrap instead?

(a) *paninis*

(b) *panini's*

5 As it loomed over me, I could feel the ....
breath on my face. It smelled terrible.

(a) *bear's*

(b) *bears'*

6 I don't believe .... toys should all be pink
– it doesn't make sense!

(a) *girl's*

(b) *girls'*

7 I met lots of people last night, but I can't
remember .... name.

(a) *anybody's*

(b) *anybodies'*

8 You should never pull a .... tail.

(a) *cat's*

(b) *cats'*

9 .... eyes reflect light in the dark.

   (a) Cat's

   (b) Cats'

10 Have you seen the .... new car? It's a Porsche!

   (a) Thompson's

   (b) Thompsons'

Choose the correct word

In each of the following pairs of sentences, choose the best word from the given word pair. You may need to change the tense, or make a word plural, depending on the context of the sentence.

advice and advise	**1** *The best .... I've ever been given is, 'Never apologise, never explain.'*
	2 Can you .... me on the best restaurants round here?

affect **and** *effect*	**3** If you stay indoors playing computer games every day, it will have a negative .... on your health. **4** Stage fright doesn't seem to .... Jessica at all – I really envy her!
complement **and** *compliment*	**5** I'm not sure that orange coat really .... your purple hair. **6** Mr Green .... me on my French pronunciation today – I must be improving.
desert **and** *dessert*	**7** We'll have apple pie and custard for .... tonight. **8** This garden will turn into a .... if you keep forgetting to water it!

imply and *infer*	**9** The lecturer looked pointedly at his watch when I sneaked into the back of the room, from which I .... he had noticed that I was late again.
	10 I don't like to ask directly for my Christmas presents – I just try to .... what I want when the subject comes up.
loose and *lose*	**11** If we keep playing like that, we just can't .... !
	12 The cat's collar is so .... that she always manages to wriggle out of it.

pore over **and** pour over	**13** Tim .... his drink .... Bethany's head and walked out. You should have seen it! **14** I love to .... old recipe books from second-hand shops.
practice **and** practise	**15** If you never .... , you'll never get any better! **16** She put her success down to hours of .... every day.
principle **and** principal	**17** My .... objective is to pass my exams. **18** 18. I'd like to be rich, but without compromising my ....

weather and *whether*	**19** *Have you seen the .... ? It's perfect for a picnic!* **20** *She didn't know .... she had passed or failed the exam because she hadn't opened the envelope yet.*

ANSWERS

Less and fewer

1	fewer	**6**	fewer
2	less	**7**	less
3	fewer	**8**	fewer
4	less	**9**	fewer
5	less	**10**	less

Adjectives and adverbs

1 *terribly*
2 *wild*
3 *delicious*
4 *rigorously*
5 *kindly*
6 *good*
7 *slowly*
8 *loudly*
9 *well*
10 *raucous*

Apostrophes in contractions

1 *It's*
2 *Your*
3 *its*
4 *they're*
5 *Their*
6 *it's*
7 *Who's*
8 *whose*
9 *there*
10 *You're*

Possessive apostrophes

1 (a) *boy's* OR (b) *boys' It depends on whether the sentence refers to one boy or more than one boy. Either option could be correct.*
2 (a) *children's*
3 (a) *Liam's*
4 (a) *paninis*
5 (a) *bear's*
6 (b) *girls'*
7 (a) *anybody's*
8 (a) *cat's*
9 (b) *Cats'*
10 (b) *Thompsons'*

Choose the correct word

1	*advice*	11	*lose*
2	*advise*	12	*loose*
3	*effect*	13	*poured/over*
4	*affect*	14	*pore over*
5	*complements*	15	*practise*
6	*complimented*	16	*practice*
7	*dessert*	17	*principal*
8	*desert*	18	*principles*
9	*inferred*	19	*weather*
10	*imply*	20	*whether*

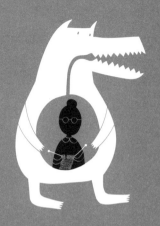

APPENDIX 1
TRICKY WORDS AND HOW TO SPELL THEM

the right way	the wrong way(s)
a lot	alot
accommodate, accommodation	accomodate, accomodation
achieve	acheive
across	accross
address	adress
anniversary	aniversary
apparently	apparantly
appearance	appearence
argument	arguement

the right way	the wrong way(s)
assassination	assasination, asassination
basically	basicly
beginning	begining
believe	beleive, belive
bizarre	bizzare
business	buisness
calendar	calender
chauffeur	chauffer
colleague	collegue

the right way	the wrong way(s)
committee	comittee, commitee
completely	completly
definitely	definately
disappear	dissapear
disappoint	dissapoint
ecstasy	ecstacy, exstasy
embarrass	embarass
emperor	emperer
environment	enviroment

the right way	the wrong way(s)
finally	finaly
fluorescent	florescent
foreseeable	forseeable
friend	freind
further	futher
glamorous	glamourous
government	goverment
guard	gaurd
happened	happend

the right way	**the wrong way(s)**
harass	harrass
honorary	honourary
humorous	humourous
immediately	immediatly
independent	independant
interrupt	interupt
irresistible	irresistable
knowledge	knowlege
manageable	managable

the right way	the wrong way(s)
necessary	neccessary
noticeable	noticable
occasion	ocassion, occassion
occurred	occured
pavilion	pavillion
persistent	persistant
piece	peice
possession	posession
precede	preceed

the right way	the wrong way(s)
publicly	publically
receive	recieve
remember	rember, remeber
resistance	resistence
separate	seperate
siege	seige
success	succes, sucess
supersede	supercede, superseed
surprise	suprise

the right way	the wrong way(s)
tendency	tendancy
tomorrow	tommorow, tommorrow
tongue	tounge
truly	truely
unforeseen	unforseen
unfortunately	unfortunatly
until	untill
weird	wierd
wherever	whereever

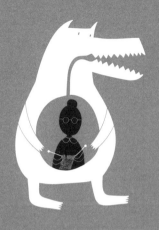

APPENDIX 2
USEFUL ABBREVIATIONS THAT WILL SPEED UP YOUR LIFE

abbreviation	description
AD	*Anno Domini* (Latin): 'in the year of the Lord' used to describe all years from Jesus Christ's birth to the present. See also CE
a.m.	*ante meridiem* (Latin): before noon
ASAP	as soon as possible
BC	Before Christ: used to describe all years before 1 AD. See also BCE
BCE	Before Common Era: used for the same purpose as BC in non-Christian contexts

abbreviation	description
BYOB	bring your own bottle, used on invitations to signify that guests should bring their own beverages
c.	*circa* (Latin): about, approximately
CE	Common Era: used for the same purpose as AD in non-Christian contexts
cf.	*confer* (Latin): compare
DIY	do it yourself: a concise way of describing crafts and home maintenance

abbreviation	description
e.g.	*exempli gratia* (Latin): for example
ETA	estimated time of arrival
etc.	*et cetera* (Latin): and other things
ibid.	*ibidem* (Latin): in the same place
i.e.	*id est* (Latin): that is
NB	*nota bene* (Latin): note well
p.m.	*post meridiem* (Latin): after noon

abbreviation	description
PS	postscript: an addition to the end of a letter or other message
PYO	pick your own: commonly used by farms where you can pick your own produce
RSVP	*Répondez s'il vous plaît*, the French for 'please reply', most often seen at the end of an invitation
viz.	*videlicet* (Latin): namely

APPENDIX 3
FREQUENTLY USED IRREGULAR VERBS

infinitive	past tense	past participle
be	was/were	been
begin	began	begun
break	broke	broken
bring	brought	brought
build	built	built
buy	bought	bought
choose	chose	chosen
come	came	come
cost	cost	cost
cut	cut	cut

infinitive	past tense	past participle
dive	dived	dived
do	did	done
draw	drew	drawn
drive	drove	driven
eat	ate	eaten
feel	felt	felt
find	found	found
freeze	froze	frozen
get	got	got [US English: gotten]
give	gave	given

infinitive	past tense	past participle
go	went	gone
grind	ground	ground
have	had	had
hear	heard	heard
hit	hit	hit
hold	held	held
keep	kept	kept
kneel	kneeled/knelt	knelt/kneeled
know	knew	known
lay	laid	laid
lead	led	led
leave	left	left

infinitive	past tense	past participle
let	let	let
lie	lay	lain
lose	lost	lost
make	made	made
mean	meant	meant
meet	met	met
pay	paid	paid
put	put	put
run	ran	run
say	said	said
see	saw	seen
sell	sold	sold

infinitive	past tense	past participle
send	sent	sent
set	set	set
sit	sat	sat
speak	spoke	spoken
spend	spent	spent
spill	spilled/spilt	spilled/spilt
split	split	split
stand	stood	stood
steal	stole	stolen
take	took	taken
teach	taught	taught
tell	told	told

infinitive	past tense	past participle
think	thought	thought
understand	understood	understood
wear	wore	worn
win	won	won
write	wrote	written

FURTHER READING

If you've enjoyed diving into the world of grammar and want to learn more, here are some recommended books and websites to investigate.

REFERENCE BOOKS

Butcher, Judith *Butcher's Copy-editing: The Cambridge Handbook for Editors, Copy-editors and Proofreaders* (2006, Cambridge University Press)

Collins Dictionaries *Easy Learning Grammar and Punctuation* (2015, Collins)

Oxford University Press *New Hart's Rules: The Oxford Style Guide* (2014, Oxford University Press)

Ritter, R. M. *New Oxford Dictionary for Writers and Editors* (2014, Oxford University Press)

Truss, Lynne *Eats, Shoots & Leaves: The Zero Tolerance Approach to Punctuation* (2009, Fourth Estate)

Waite, Maurice *New Oxford Spelling Dictionary* (2014, Oxford University Press)

ONLINE STYLE GUIDES

BBC Bitesize – Spelling, punctuation and grammar: www.bbc.co.uk/education/topics/z2b2tyc

BBC News Style Guide: www.bbc.co.uk/academy/journalism/news-style-guide

The Economist Style Guide: www.economist.com/styleguide/introduction

The Guardian and *Observer* Style Guide: www.theguardian.com/info/series/guardian-and-observer-style-guide

The Telegraph Style Book: www.telegraph.co.uk/topics/about-us/style-book

NOTES

....

....

....

....

....

....

....

....

....

....

....

....

....

....

....

....

....

....

....

....
....
....
....
....
....
....
....
....
....
....
....
....
....
....
....
....
....
....

....
....
....
....
....
....
....
....
....
....
....
....
....
....
....
....
....
....
....
....
....
....

....

....

....

....

....

....

....

....

....

....

....

....

....

....

....

....

....

....

....

....

....

KNOWLEDGE

STUFF YOU OUGHT TO KNOW

RAY HAMILTON

KNOWLEDGE
Stuff You Ought to Know

Ray Hamilton

£7.99
Hardback
ISBN: 978-1-84953-889-3

This outrageously informative book is packed full of fascinating nuggets of history, science, literature, technology, sports, geography, culture and miscellanea from every corner of the world – enough mind-blowing trivia to ensure you're never short of a jaw-dropping conversation starter (or stopper) again.

A LITERARY FEAST

FEAST

*Recipes inspired by
novels, poems and plays*

JENNIFER BARCLAY

A LITERARY FEAST
Recipes Inspired by Novels, Poems and Plays

Jennifer Barclay

£9.99
Hardback
ISBN: 978-1-84953-737-7

Prepare your senses for a feast of delicious food scenes in literature accompanied with recipes to bring them to life in your very own kitchen.

This book is perfect for anyone who enjoys spending their days with a book in one hand and a saucepan in the other.

Have you enjoyed this book?
If so, why not write a review on
your favourite website?

If you're interested in finding out more
about our books, find us on Facebook
at Summersdale Publishers and follow
us on Twitter at @Summersdale.

Thanks very much for buying
this Summersdale book.

www.summersdale.com